MacBook Seniors Guide

A Complete Step-by-Step Manual for Non-Tech-Savvy Users to Navigate and Enjoy Modern Technology with Ease

Ronny G. Mason

TABLE OF CONTENT

INTRODUCTION

Welcome to MacBook: A Perfect Companion for Seniors

Congratulations on choosing a MacBook! You've made an excellent decision, especially as a senior, because MacBooks are known for being easy to use, reliable, and secure. Whether you're looking to stay in touch with loved ones, manage your daily tasks, explore new interests, or simply enjoy entertainment, your MacBook is a versatile companion designed to make your digital experience comfortable, safe, and enjoyable.

This guide is tailored specifically for seniors, ensuring that every step, tip, and explanation is clear and simple. You won't have to deal with confusing technical jargon. Instead, you'll learn practical skills that allow you to confidently navigate your MacBook.

About macOS: Your Friendly Operating System

Your MacBook runs on a special software called macOS. Think of macOS as the friendly neighborhood guide inside your computer, helping you easily access everything you need. With intuitive features, simple navigation, and built-in support tools, macOS is thoughtfully designed to accommodate users of all ages, including seniors.

Throughout this guide, you'll get familiar with macOS, learning how to perform tasks efficiently, set up your preferences, manage your security, and use various applications effortlessly. macOS updates regularly to protect you from digital threats and ensure your MacBook continues to run smoothly.

How to Use This Guide Effectively

This guide is structured to be easy-to-follow. You can read it from beginning to end or jump directly to the chapters that interest you most. Each chapter clearly outlines what you'll learn and provides step-by-step instructions that you can follow at your own pace.

We've also included two bonus chapters for you, offering valuable resources and a handy quick-reference guide to keyboard shortcuts, further enhancing your MacBook experience.

Remember, there's no rush—take your time to explore, experiment, and enjoy your MacBook. Let's get started!

GETTING STARTED WITH YOUR MACBOOK

Unboxing your MacBook

Congratulations! The exciting moment of unboxing your new MacBook has arrived. Here's what you'll typically find inside the box:

- **Your MacBook:** Beautifully designed, lightweight, and ready for you to explore.
- **Power Adapter and Charging Cable:** Essential for charging your MacBook.
- **Documentation:** Quick start guide, warranty information, and stickers.

Take your time to carefully remove each item from the packaging. It's a good idea to keep the box and packaging materials safe, just in case you need them later for storage or service purposes.

When handling your MacBook for the first time:

1. Place it on a stable, flat surface.
2. Open the lid gently. Your MacBook might automatically start up when you open it.
3. Connect the charging cable to your MacBook and plug the power adapter into an electrical outlet to ensure it's fully charged for the initial setup.

Enjoy the first moments with your MacBook as you prepare to explore everything it has to offer!

Understanding what's included in the box

Let's open the box together and explore what's inside. Here's what you'll typically find:

- **Your MacBook**: This sleek, lightweight laptop is your gateway to everything digital—perfect for staying in touch with family, managing tasks, or simply enjoying your favorite movies and music.
- **Charging Adapter and USB-C Cable**: Think of these like your MacBook's power source. The adapter plugs into your wall socket, and the cable connects the adapter to your MacBook, ensuring it stays charged and ready to use.
- **Documentation**: Inside, you'll find a Quick Start Guide, warranty details, and some Apple stickers. Keep these handy just in case you have questions later.

Feel free to take your time unboxing—it's exciting and worth savoring! It's also helpful to keep the packaging somewhere safe in case you ever need it later.

Initial setup & Apple ID creation

Now, let's turn on your MacBook and get started. Here's what you do step-by-step:

1. **Open the Lid and Turn On**: Gently open the lid. Your MacBook might automatically start. If not, simply press the power button.
2. **Choose Your Language**: A friendly setup assistant will appear. Choose your language from the list—this ensures everything is clear and comfortable for you.
3. **Select Your Country or Region**: Pick your country or region so your MacBook shows the right settings.
4. **Connect to Wi-Fi**: Your MacBook will ask to join your home Wi-Fi network. Select your network and type in your Wi-Fi password. (Don't worry—this is usually written on your internet router or provided by your service provider.)
5. **Set Up Location Services**: The setup assistant might ask if you want to enable location services. This helps your MacBook offer useful information, like local weather. It's completely safe to say "yes" here.

6. **Create or Sign in to Your Apple ID**:
    - ○ **What's an Apple ID?** Think of it as your personal passport to the Apple universe. It lets you use services like FaceTime, the App Store, and iCloud, which securely stores photos, documents, and more.
    - ○ If you already have an Apple ID from an iPhone or iPad, you can simply sign in.
    - ○ If you're new to Apple, creating an ID is easy. Just follow the simple instructions on your screen. You'll need your email address and a secure password (more on that below!).

Don't worry if technology isn't your strong suit—this step is simpler than it sounds, and the assistant guides you through clearly and patiently.

Account security: Passwords, Passkeys, and Face ID/Touch ID

Now, let's quickly cover some basics to keep your MacBook safe and secure. Think of your MacBook as your home—security matters, but it doesn't need to be complicated.

- **Passwords**: Your password is like the key to your front door—choose one that is strong, memorable to you, but not obvious to others. It helps protect your personal information.
- **Passkeys**: Passkeys are like digital house keys. They securely simplify signing in to websites and apps without needing to remember complicated passwords.
- **Face ID / Touch ID**: Imagine unlocking your door simply by looking at it or touching it—this is exactly what Face ID (facial recognition) or Touch ID (fingerprint recognition) does. It's quick, secure, and very convenient.

Helpful Tip: Choose passwords that combine letters, numbers, and symbols, and avoid using easily guessed information like birthdays or names of family members. And don't worry—if passwords feel overwhelming, Face ID or Touch ID makes security easier than ever.

Now you're all set! Take your time, enjoy each step, and remember—you can always come back to this guide whenever you need help.

NAVIGATING YOUR MACBOOK

Basic MacBook navigation (Dock, Finder, Desktop, Menu Bar)

Let's explore how your MacBook works. Here are the basics you'll use every day:

Desktop: Think of this as your home screen. It's where you land after turning on your MacBook, showing icons for easy access to files and apps.

Dock: This bar at the bottom of your screen is like a handy shelf. It holds apps you use most, such as Safari for browsing the internet or Mail for emails.

Finder: Finder is like your filing cabinet. It helps you quickly find and organize your files, documents, and folders.

Menu Bar: Located at the top, this bar gives you quick access to important settings like battery life, Wi-Fi connection, and date/time

Trackpad gestures and mouse settings

Your MacBook's trackpad is like your mouse—only easier and smoother. Here's how to use it effectively:

Click: Press down gently anywhere on the trackpad to select or open something.

Right-Click: Click with two fingers gently to see extra options, similar to a right-click on a traditional mouse.

Scroll: Slide two fingers up or down gently to move through documents or web pages, like scrolling down a newspaper page.

Zoom: Place two fingers on the trackpad and pinch them together or apart, just as you would to zoom on a smartphone or tablet.

Swipe Between Apps: Move three fingers left or right to switch quickly between open applications, like flipping pages of a magazine.

Open Launchpad: Pinch with your thumb and three fingers to open Launchpad, showing all your apps clearly in one place.

Adjusting Trackpad and Mouse Settings

Want to customize your trackpad or mouse settings? Follow these simple steps:

1. Click the Apple icon () in the top-left corner.
2. Select System Preferences from the menu.
3. Click on Trackpad or Mouse.
4. Here, you can adjust:

- Tracking Speed: How fast the cursor moves.
- Click Pressure: How much pressure is needed for clicking.
- Scroll Direction: Choose the scroll direction that feels most natural for you.

Adjusting display & accessibility settings (text size, contrast, zoom features)

Making your MacBook screen comfortable for your eyes is essential, and Apple has made it easy. Let's carefully explore how to adjust these settings:

Adjusting Text Size and Screen Resolution

To make words and icons easier to see:

1. Click the Apple icon () in the top-left corner.
2. Choose **System Preferences**, then click on **Displays**.
3. Select **Scaled**, and you'll see several options. Choosing a larger text size or lower resolution makes everything bigger and clearer. Feel free to experiment until you find the setting that's most comfortable.

Changing Screen Brightness

Adjust brightness quickly and easily:

- Simply press the brightness keys located at the top row of your keyboard (they look like suns).
- Or, you can go to **System Preferences**, then click **Displays**, and use the slider to adjust brightness to your liking.

Adjusting Screen Contrast

To enhance screen clarity:

1. Go to **System Preferences**, then click **Accessibility**.
2. Choose **Display** on the left.
3. Here, you can adjust contrast with a simple slider, making text and images easier to distinguish.

Using Zoom Features

If you ever find text or images too small to see clearly, your MacBook has a wonderful zoom feature:

1. In **System Preferences**, click on **Accessibility**.
2. Select **Zoom** from the menu.
3. Check the box to enable zoom. You can choose between various zoom styles:
   - **Keyboard shortcuts**: Press `Option + Command + =` to zoom in and `Option + Command + -` to zoom out.
   - **Scroll Gesture**: Hold the Control key and scroll with two fingers on the trackpad to zoom easily.

Exploring Additional Accessibility Tools

Your MacBook has built-in tools to assist you even more:

- **VoiceOver**: Your MacBook can read aloud text on your screen, helpful if your eyes need a rest.
- **Speech to Text**: Dictate what you want to type instead of using the keyboard, handy if typing is difficult or uncomfortable.
- **Cursor Size**: Make your mouse pointer bigger and easier to find by adjusting the cursor size under Accessibility settings.

STAYING CONNECTED

Connecting to Wi-Fi & managing network settings

Staying connected to the internet is essential for enjoying your MacBook fully. Let's walk through connecting to Wi-Fi and managing your network settings step-by-step:

Connecting to Wi-Fi

1. Look at the top-right corner of your screen, and click on the **Wi-Fi icon** (it looks like curved lines forming a fan shape).
2. You will see a list of available Wi-Fi networks. Select your home network's name (also known as the SSID). Usually, this name is printed on your internet router or provided by your internet company.
3. Enter the Wi-Fi password when asked. This password is typically printed on your router or provided by your internet company.
4. Click **Join**. Your MacBook will connect automatically in a few seconds.

Once connected, you'll see the Wi-Fi icon turn solid black—indicating you're successfully online!

Managing Network Settings

Sometimes you might need to change or check your network settings. Here's how:

1. Click on the Apple icon () at the top-left corner of your screen.
2. Select **System Preferences** and click on **Network**.
3. You'll see various connection options, such as Wi-Fi, Ethernet, and Bluetooth.
   - **Wi-Fi**: Click to check connection status, choose another network, or manage advanced settings.

- Advanced: Click this button to see more settings, including saved networks, DNS, and IP settings.

4. From the **Advanced** menu, you can:
   - **Manage Known Networks**: Remove or rearrange networks your MacBook connects to automatically.
   - **Renew DHCP Lease**: If you're experiencing connection issues, clicking this may help your MacBook reconnect smoothly.

Email setup (Apple Mail app)

Setting up your email is easy and convenient with Apple's built-in Mail app. Let's get you started step-by-step:

Adding an Email Account

1. Click the **Mail** icon in your Dock (it looks like a postage stamp). If it's not there, open Launchpad and click Mail.
2. When you open Mail for the first time, it'll ask you to choose an email provider (like Gmail, Yahoo, or iCloud). Select your email provider.
3. Enter your email address and click **Next**.
4. Enter your password (the one you normally use to access your email).
5. Click **Sign In**.
6. Choose the apps you'd like to use with your email account. Usually, Mail is automatically checked. You can leave the default settings and click **Done**.

Your emails will now appear in your inbox, and you're ready to send and receive messages!

Sending and Receiving Emails

- **Sending an Email**: Click **New Message** at the top-left corner. Enter your recipient's email, type your subject and message, then click **Send**.
- **Reading Emails**: Simply click an email from your inbox to read it.
- **Replying**: Click the **Reply** arrow in the email itself, type your response, and click **Send**.

FaceTime & video calls

FaceTime is Apple's built-in app for making easy and enjoyable video calls with family and friends. Whether they're across town or around the world, FaceTime helps you see and talk to each other clearly and simply. Let's go step-by-step on how to use FaceTime.

Setting Up FaceTime

FaceTime is already installed on your MacBook, so getting started is straightforward:

1. Find the **FaceTime app** (the green icon with a white video camera). You can find it on your Dock or in Launchpad.
2. Click the FaceTime icon to open the app.
3. Sign in with your Apple ID if prompted. Use the same Apple ID you created earlier or use on your iPhone or iPad.

Making a FaceTime Call

Making a video call with FaceTime is simple and fun:

1. Once FaceTime is open, you'll see a search box at the top. Type the name, email address, or phone number of the person you'd like to call.
2. A list will appear with matching contacts. Click the name or number of the person you're calling.
3. To start a video call, click the **video camera icon** next to their name. To make an audio-only call, click the **phone icon**.
4. Wait a moment, and your call will start ringing. Once your friend or family member answers, you'll see their smiling face on your screen!

Receiving a FaceTime Call

When someone calls you, you'll hear a pleasant ringing sound, and a notification will appear on your screen:

- Click the **green Accept** button to answer and start chatting.
- If you can't answer right away, click the **red Decline** button. You can always call them back later.

Helpful Tips for a Great FaceTime Experience

- **Lighting**: Sit facing a light source like a window or lamp, making it easier for others to see your face clearly.
- **Sound**: Ensure your MacBook volume is at a comfortable level, using the keys at the top of your keyboard to adjust.
- **Camera Position**: Adjust your screen angle slightly until you appear comfortably centered in the camera view.

Group FaceTime Calls

FaceTime also allows you to chat with several people at once—great for family gatherings or catching up with multiple friends:

1. Open FaceTime and click **New FaceTime**.
2. Type and select each contact you want to include.
3. Click the **video camera icon** to start the call.

Everyone invited can join, creating a warm and interactive experience.

Messaging & using iMessage

Staying in touch with your loved ones is easy and enjoyable with Apple's Messages app. Let's explore how to use iMessage step-by-step, making your communication seamless and fun.

Getting Started with iMessage

1. **Open the Messages App**: Click the Messages icon (a blue speech bubble) on your Dock. If it's not visible, click Launchpad and select Messages.
2. **Sign In with Your Apple ID**: If prompted, enter your Apple ID and password to activate iMessage. This ensures your messages sync across your Apple devices.

Sending and Receiving Messages

- **Starting a New Conversation**:
  - Click the **Compose New Message** button (it looks like a pencil and paper icon) at the top-left corner.
  - Type the name or phone number of your contact. Your MacBook will suggest contacts as you type.
  - Type your message in the text box at the bottom of the window.
  - Press **Return** (Enter) on your keyboard to send the message.
- **Reading Messages**:
  - New messages will appear on the left side of the Messages window. Click any conversation to open it and read the latest messages.

Sending Photos, Videos, and Files

You can also share memorable moments or useful files with ease:

- Click the **Photos** button (small image icon) to send pictures from your Photos app.
- Drag and drop any file directly into the conversation window to send it quickly.

Adding Emojis and Fun Reactions

Make your conversations lively and personal with emojis or reactions:

- **Emojis**: Click the smiley face icon at the bottom of your message box. Choose from many emojis to express yourself!
- **Reactions**: Click and hold any message you received, and select a reaction (like a thumbs up or heart) to quickly respond without typing.

Using Group Conversations

Stay connected with family groups or friends in one chat:

1. Start a new message, then enter multiple contacts.
2. Send your message, and everyone in the group can respond. It's perfect for family updates or chatting with friends!

Managing Your Messages

- **Deleting a Conversation**: Right-click (or hold the Control key and click) the conversation you want to delete, then select **Delete Conversation**.
- **Muting Conversations**: Click the conversation, then click **Details** at the top right corner and select **Do Not Disturb** to mute notifications.

EVERYDAY APPS & FEATURES

Safari: Safe internet browsing, bookmarks, and privacy

Getting Started with Safari

- **Opening Safari**:
  - ○ Click the Safari icon (compass-shaped) in your Dock or open it through Launchpad.
- **Visiting Websites**:
  - ○ Click on the address bar at the top, type the website name (such as "www.google.com"), and press Enter.

Safe and Private Browsing

Safari includes features designed to protect your privacy and security:

- **Private Browsing**:
  - ○ To keep your browsing history private, click **File** in the menu bar and select **New Private Window**. In this mode, Safari won't save your browsing history, cookies, or search history.
- **Managing Your Browsing History**:
  - ○ Click **History** in the menu bar to view websites you previously visited or to clear your history to keep your browsing habits private.
- **Security Warnings**:
  - ○ Safari will alert you if it detects suspicious websites, helping keep your personal information safe.

Bookmarking Your Favorite Websites

Bookmarks let you quickly revisit websites you enjoy:

- **Adding a Bookmark**:
    1. Go to the website you'd like to bookmark.
    2. Click the **Share button** (a square with an arrow pointing up) in the toolbar, then select **Add Bookmark**.
    3. Name your bookmark, choose a location (such as the Bookmarks Bar), and click **Add**.
- **Accessing Your Bookmarks**:
    1. Your bookmarks appear in the **Bookmarks Bar** below the address bar, or click **Bookmarks** in the menu bar to see the complete list.
- **Managing Bookmarks**:
    1. Click **Bookmarks** > **Edit Bookmarks** from the menu bar.
    2. You can organize, rename, or delete bookmarks easily here.

Adjusting Privacy Settings

Safari makes it easy to manage privacy and ensure your data stays safe:

1. Click **Safari** in the menu bar and select **Settings**.
2. Choose the **Privacy** tab.
3. Here you can:
    - Block or allow cookies (small files websites use to remember your preferences).
    - Limit websites from tracking your activities.

Helpful Tips for Secure Browsing

- Always double-check the website address (URL) before entering personal details.
- Look for a lock icon 🔒 in the address bar, meaning the website is secure.
- Never click suspicious or unexpected links received in emails or messages.

Using Calendar, Reminders, and Notes effectively

Using Calendar, Reminders, and Notes Effectively

Your MacBook comes with powerful tools to help you stay organized in your daily life. These include the **Calendar**, **Reminders**, and **Notes** apps. They're simple to use and incredibly helpful for keeping track of appointments, to-do lists, and your personal thoughts or ideas.

Using the Calendar App

The Calendar app helps you keep track of important dates and appointments.

To open Calendar:

1. Click the **Calendar** icon from your Dock (it looks like a little red and white calendar).
2. If it's not in the Dock, open **Launchpad**, then click **Calendar**.

Adding an Event:

1. Click the **plus (+)** button at the top-left corner.
2. A small window will appear. Enter a title, like "Doctor's Appointment."
3. Choose the date and time.
4. You can also add a location (like "Downtown Clinic") and set a reminder so your Mac notifies you in advance.
5. Click **Add** when you're finished.

Viewing Your Calendar:

- Switch between **Day**, **Week**, **Month**, or **Year** view using the buttons at the top of the window.
- Click on any date to see what's planned.

Tip: You can sync your calendar with your iPhone or iPad so you can view your schedule on all your devices.

Using the Reminders App

The Reminders app is perfect for keeping track of tasks like grocery lists, errands, or medication schedules.

To open Reminders:

1. Click the **Reminders** icon from the Dock, or find it using Launchpad.

Creating a Reminder:

1. Click **New Reminder** in the bottom-left corner.
2. Type what you want to remember (e.g., "Take blood pressure meds at 8 AM").
3. Click the small "i" (information button) to:
   - Set a **time and date** to get a reminder notification.
   - Mark the task as high priority if it's urgent.

Organizing Reminders:

- Create different lists for different tasks: like "Shopping," "Chores," or "Appointments."
- When you complete a task, click the checkbox next to it. It's a satisfying way to stay on top of things!

Using the Notes App

The Notes app is your digital notebook. You can use it to jot down ideas, recipes, passwords, or even journal entries.

To open Notes:

1. Click the **Notes** icon in the Dock or open it from Launchpad.

Creating a New Note:

1. Click the **New Note** button (square with a pencil) at the top.
2. Type anything you'd like to remember or save.

Organizing Your Notes:

- Click **Folders** to create categories (like "Recipes," "Travel Plans," or "Important Info").
- Drag notes into folders to keep everything tidy.

Formatting Text:

- You can bold, underline, or add bullet points by clicking the format button at the top of your note.

Bonus Feature:

- You can also insert images, scanned documents, and checklists into your notes for extra usefulness.

Photos App: Managing, editing, and sharing pictures

Your MacBook's **Photos app** is a wonderful place to store, enjoy, and share your favorite memories. Whether it's photos from your phone, email, or camera, the Photos app helps you keep everything organized and beautiful.

Opening the Photos App

1. Click the **Photos** icon (it looks like a colorful flower) in your Dock.
2. If it's not there, click **Launchpad** (the rocket icon), then select **Photos** from the list.

Viewing Your Photos

- When the app opens, you'll see your **Library** — this is where all your pictures are stored.
- Photos are usually sorted by **date** and organized into sections like **Years, Months, Days**, and **All Photos**.
- Click any photo to open it and view it in full screen.

Importing Photos

You can easily add new pictures to your MacBook:

1. Connect your camera, iPhone, or USB drive.
2. The Photos app will ask if you want to **Import** pictures. Click **Import All**, or select specific ones.

Your photos will now appear in your Library.

Creating Albums to Stay Organized

Albums help you group photos together—just like a physical photo album:

1. In the left sidebar, click **My Albums**.
2. Click the **plus (+) button**, then select **Album**.
3. Name your album (for example: "Family Reunion 2023").
4. Drag and drop photos into the album.

This keeps everything tidy and easy to find.

Editing Your Photos

Want to brighten a photo or crop it? It's simple!

1. Double-click the photo you want to edit.
2. Click **Edit** in the top-right corner.
3. You'll see basic tools like:
    - **Auto-Enhance**: One click to make your photo look better.
    - **Crop**: Trim unwanted edges.
    - **Filters**: Add different looks or moods to your photo.
    - **Adjust**: Change brightness, color, or contrast.
4. If you don't like the changes, click **Revert to Original** anytime.

Feel free to play around—your original photo is always saved!

Sharing Photos with Family and Friends

1. Select the photo (or multiple photos) you want to share.
2. Click the **Share** button (a square with an arrow pointing up).
3. Choose how you want to share:
    - **Email**: Send the photo directly by email.
    - **Messages**: Send it to someone using iMessage.
    - **AirDrop**: Instantly send it to nearby Apple devices.

Sharing pictures is a lovely way to stay connected and brighten someone's day.

Searching for Photos

You can find pictures quickly by using the search bar:

- Type in a place, date, or even the name of a person (if your photos are labeled).
- The Photos app will show matching results in seconds.

Final Tip

Don't worry about making mistakes — you can't ruin your photos. The Photos app always keeps your original image safe. So go ahead and explore, enjoy your memories, and feel proud of how easily you can manage your digital photo collection!

Music, Podcasts, and entertainment apps

Your MacBook isn't just a tool—it's also a source of joy and relaxation. With a few clicks, you can listen to your favorite music, enjoy interesting podcasts, and watch movies or shows.

Listening to Music with Apple Music

Apple Music is your built-in music player. It gives you access to millions of songs, albums, and playlists.

1. Click the **Music** app in your Dock (it looks like a musical note).
2. If this is your first time opening it, you may be asked to sign in with your Apple ID.
3. From here, you can:
   - Browse music by genre, artist, or album.
   - Search for specific songs using the search bar.
   - Play curated playlists for different moods (like relaxing or energizing).

You can also create your own playlists by clicking **File > New > Playlist**.

If you subscribe to Apple Music, you'll have access to streaming music. If not, you can still listen to songs you've purchased or imported from CDs.

Enjoying Podcasts

Podcasts are like radio shows on any topic you can imagine—news, storytelling, interviews, education, and more.

1. Open the **Podcasts** app (it looks like a purple icon with a microphone symbol).
2. Browse featured shows or search for a topic you enjoy.
3. Click **Follow** to subscribe to a podcast you like.
4. Click an episode and then press **Play** to listen.

You can pause anytime, skip ahead, or go back. Many seniors enjoy podcasts during walks or while doing chores around the house!

Watching Videos with the TV App

Want to watch a movie or TV show? Your MacBook makes it easy.

1. Open the **TV** app (a black icon with a white Apple logo and "TV").
2. Here, you can:
   ○ Watch shows and movies you've bought or rented.
   ○ Subscribe to streaming services like Apple TV+, Netflix, or Hulu.
   ○ Browse popular titles in the **Watch Now** section.

To rent or buy something, you'll need your Apple ID and payment method set up.

Using Safari for Online Entertainment

If you prefer using websites:

- Open **Safari** (the blue compass icon).
- Visit websites like **YouTube** for free videos or **Spotify** for music.
- You can bookmark your favorite sites for quick access.

Accessing news and weather

Your MacBook can help you stay informed and prepared, whether you want to catch up on the latest headlines or check tomorrow's weather forecast. Here's how to make the most of your news and weather tools.

Using the News App

The built-in **News** app gathers stories from reliable sources and presents them in an easy-to-read format.

1. Open the **News** app (it looks like a red "N" on a white background) from your Dock or Launchpad.
2. When you open the app, you'll see **Top Stories** and **Trending News**.
3. You can scroll through headlines and click on a story to read the full article.
4. Use the **Search** bar to look up news about topics or people you care about.
5. You can also choose topics to follow, such as health, politics, or entertainment. The app will then show more stories that match your interests.

Helpful Tip: If you like a news source (like BBC or CNN), you can choose to follow it so their articles appear more often.

Checking the Weather

To check the weather, you can use the built-in **Weather** app or search online. Here are both options:

Option 1: Using the Weather App

1. Open **Launchpad** and type "Weather" in the search bar.
2. Click on the **Weather** app.
3. You'll see your local forecast, including temperature, hourly updates, and a 10-day forecast.

4. To see weather in another location (maybe where your children live), click the **Add** button (+) and enter the city's name.

Option 2: Checking Weather in Safari

1. Open **Safari** (the blue compass icon).
2. Type in "[your city] weather" (for example, "Chicago weather") and press **Return**.
3. The current weather, including the temperature and forecast, will appear right at the top of the search results.

Add Weather to Your Notification Center

You can also quickly view the weather from your Notification Center:

1. Click the Date and Time in the top-right corner of your screen.
2. Scroll through your widgets to find the Weather widget.
3. If it's not there, click Edit Widgets, find Weather, and add it.

PRODUCTIVITY & ORGANIZATION

Creating and editing documents (Pages, Microsoft Word)

Whether you're writing a letter to a friend, making a shopping list, or typing up your memoirs, your MacBook makes it easy to create and edit documents using either **Pages** (Apple's free word processor) or **Microsoft Word** (a popular program available by subscription).

Using Pages (Free and Built-in)

Pages is a great choice for beginners. It's simple, elegant, and already installed on your Mac.

Opening Pages:

1. Click on the **Pages** icon in your Dock (it looks like a pen on paper). If you don't see it there, click **Launchpad** and search for "Pages."
2. When it opens, click **New Document**.
3. Choose a **Blank document** to start fresh or select from templates like letters, newsletters, or reports.
4. Click **Choose** to open your document.

Typing and Formatting:

- Start typing your content just like you would on a typewriter.
- Use the top toolbar to:
    - Change fonts, text size, and colors
    - Make text bold or italic
    - Align text (left, center, right)
    - Add bullet points or numbered lists

Inserting Extras:

You can also add:

- **Photos** from your Mac (click the **Media** button)
- **Shapes, charts, or tables** (great for visual content)

Saving Your Work:

1. Click **File > Save**.
2. Give your document a name (like "Grocery List" or "Family Letter").
3. Choose a location to save—"Documents" or "Desktop" is a good choice.
4. Click **Save.**

Pages also saves your work automatically as you go.

Printing:

- Go to **File > Print**.
- Review how the document will look.
- Click **Print** to create a hard copy.

Using Microsoft Word (If Installed)

If you're familiar with Word from a past job or prefer its layout, it works great on a Mac too.

Getting Started:

1. Open **Microsoft Word** from your Dock or Launchpad.
2. Sign in with a Microsoft account (required for full features).
3. Click **Blank Document** to start, or choose from templates.

Writing and Editing:

- Begin typing your content.

- Use the ribbon toolbar at the top to:
  - Format text (font, color, size)
  - Add headings, bullet points, or styles
  - Insert pictures or tables

Saving Documents:

1. Click **File > Save As**.
2. Enter a name and choose a folder to save it in.
3. Click **Save.**

Tip: Word documents save with the file extension .docx, which is widely recognized and great for sharing.

Printing and Exporting:

- Click **File > Print** to print your document.
- You can also export your document as a PDF by clicking **File > Export > PDF**.

Opening, Editing, and Sharing Documents

To open documents again:

1. Open Pages or Word.
2. Click **Open Recent** or **Open**, then select your file.

To share a document:

- Click the **Share** button (a square with an arrow) or go to **File > Share**.
- Choose **Mail**, **Messages**, or **AirDrop** to send it easily.

Choosing Between Pages and Word

- **Pages** is great if you want something clean, easy, and free.
- **Word** is better if you need to work with people using Windows PCs or if you're already used to it.

Spreadsheets and finances (Numbers, Excel basics)

Whether you want to track household expenses, create a simple budget, or organize information in rows and columns, your MacBook has two great tools: **Numbers** (Apple's free spreadsheet app) and **Microsoft Excel** (a widely used spreadsheet program).

Let's take a closer look at both, step-by-step.

Getting Started with Numbers (Free and Built-In)

Numbers is easy to use, visually appealing, and already installed on your Mac.

Opening Numbers:

1. Click the **Numbers** icon in your Dock (it looks like a green bar chart). If it's not there, go to **Launchpad** and search for "Numbers."
2. Click **New Document**.
3. Choose from a variety of templates. For beginners, the **Blank** template or **Simple Budget** is a great place to start.
4. Click **Choose** to open your spreadsheet.

Understanding the Layout:

- The spreadsheet is made of **rows** (horizontal) and **columns** (vertical).
- Each box is called a **cell**. You can click a cell and start typing to enter data (like a number or word).

Basic Tasks:

- **Enter Text or Numbers**: Click a cell and type. Press **Return** to move to the cell below.

- **Simple Math**: Click a cell, type =, then a formula like =5+5 or =A1+B1 (this adds the numbers in cells A1 and B1).
- **Formatting Cells**: Use the top toolbar to make text bold, change colors, or format numbers as currency.

Creating a Simple Budget:

1. Label the first column with expense categories (like Rent, Groceries, Utilities).
2. In the second column, list your monthly costs.
3. Add a row at the bottom that sums everything up:
   - Click the cell where you want the total.
   - Type =SUM(B1:B5) (adjust the range based on your rows).
   - Press **Return** to see the total.

Saving and Printing:

- Click **File > Save** to name and store your spreadsheet.
- Click **File > Print** to get a hard copy.

Using Microsoft Excel (If Installed)

If you're more comfortable with Excel or already have it installed, it offers similar tools with a slightly different layout.

Opening Excel:

1. Click the **Excel** icon in your Dock or open it from **Launchpad**.
2. Sign in with a Microsoft account, if needed.
3. Choose **Blank Workbook** or a template (such as Personal Budget).

Basic Excel Tasks:

- **Enter data** into cells by clicking and typing.

- Use the **Formula Bar** above the grid to enter calculations.
- Format text, numbers, or apply cell colors using the toolbar ribbon.

Common Excel Formulas:

- `=SUM(A1:A5)` — adds a list of numbers.
- `=AVERAGE(B1:B5)` — gives the average of selected numbers.
- `=A1*B1` — multiplies the values in two cells.

Charts and Tables:

1. Highlight the data you want to turn into a chart.
2. Click the **Insert** tab and choose a chart type (like bar or pie).
3. Excel will display the chart right in your sheet.

Saving and Exporting:

- Save your spreadsheet by going to **File > Save As**.
- Export to PDF or share it by email.

Choosing Between Numbers and Excel

- **Numbers** is best for beginners, especially for simple personal tasks. It's free and user-friendly.
- **Excel** is more advanced, great for more detailed financial planning or if you're used to it from work.

Either way, you'll find managing finances on your MacBook both practical and empowering.

Printing & managing printers

Printing from your MacBook is a breeze once everything is set up. Whether you're printing a letter, a grocery list, or a family photo, your MacBook can connect to a printer wirelessly or by cable. Here's a simple guide to help you print with confidence.

Connecting a Printer to Your MacBook

Option 1: Wireless Printer

If your printer supports Wi-Fi:

1. Turn on your printer and make sure it's connected to the same Wi-Fi network as your MacBook.
2. On your MacBook, click the **Apple menu ()** and go to **System Preferences**.
3. Click **Printers & Scanners**.
4. Click the **plus (+) button** to add a printer.
5. Wait a moment while your MacBook finds the printer. When it appears, click it and then click **Add**.

Option 2: USB Cable Connection

If you're using a wired printer:

1. Plug the printer into your MacBook using a USB cable.
2. Your Mac will usually recognize the printer automatically.
3. If it doesn't, follow the same steps above to add it manually from **Printers & Scanners**.

What is AirPrint?

AirPrint is Apple's built-in wireless printing technology. It allows you to print from your MacBook (or iPhone/iPad) without needing to install any drivers or extra software.

If your printer supports AirPrint:

- Your Mac will detect it automatically when it's on the same Wi-Fi network.
- Just choose the printer from the list when printing—no setup required!

Look for the "AirPrint" label on your printer box or manual. Many modern printers include this feature.

Printing a Document

Once your printer is connected, printing is simple:

1. Open the document you want to print (in Pages, Word, Numbers, etc.).
2. Click **File** in the top menu.
3. Select **Print**, or press Command + P on your keyboard.
4. In the print dialog box, you can:
   - Choose which printer to use
   - Select how many copies
   - Choose specific pages to print (if you don't want to print the whole document)
   - Adjust layout options like paper size or orientation
5. When everything looks good, click **Print**.

Printing Photos from the Photos App

To print a favorite picture:

1. Open the **Photos** app.
2. Find and click the photo you want to print.
3. Click **File > Print** or press Command + P.
4. In the print options, you can:
   - Choose the size of the photo
   - Select layout options (like borderless)
   - Pick how many copies to print
5. Click **Print** when ready.

Tip: For the best results, use photo paper and check that your printer settings are optimized for photo printing.

Creating PDF Files Instead of Printing

Sometimes, you may want to save your document as a digital file instead of printing it on paper. PDF files are great for sharing or saving without using ink or paper.

To create a PDF:

1. Open your document.
2. Go to **File > Print**.
3. In the bottom-left corner of the print dialog box, click the **PDF** button.
4. Choose **Save as PDF**.
5. Enter a file name and choose where to save it.
6. Click **Save**.

Managing Printer Settings

To change default settings or troubleshoot:

1. Go to **System Preferences > Printers & Scanners**.
2. Click on your printer's name.
3. From here, you can:
   - **Set default options** (like double-sided printing)
   - **Open Print Queue** to see or cancel print jobs
   - **Check printer status** (such as low ink or paper jams)

Troubleshooting Tips

If your printer isn't responding:

- **Check Wi-Fi**: Make sure both your MacBook and the printer are on the same network.

- **Restart Devices**: Restart both the printer and your Mac.
- **Update Software**: Go to **System Preferences > Software Update** to install any updates.
- **Check Cables**: For wired printers, ensure cables are properly plugged in.

Organizing files and folders clearly

As you begin creating documents, downloading files, or saving pictures, it's important to keep everything organized. Think of your MacBook like a digital filing cabinet—it works best when everything is neatly sorted into the right folders.

Here's how to manage files and folders easily and clearly.

Understanding the Finder

Finder is the tool you'll use to access and organize everything on your Mac.

- Click the **Finder icon** (it looks like a blue smiling face) in your Dock.
- This opens a window where you can see your files, folders, downloads, pictures, and more.
- On the left sidebar, you'll find quick links like **Documents**, **Desktop**, **Downloads**, and **Applications**.

Creating a New Folder

Folders help keep similar files together:

1. Open **Finder**.
2. Navigate to the location where you want to create the folder (for example, inside **Documents**).
3. Click **File > New Folder** in the top menu—or right-click and select **New Folder**.
4. A folder will appear named **Untitled Folder**. Click on the name and type a new one (like "Travel Plans" or "Recipes").

Moving Files into Folders

To keep things tidy:

1. Click and drag any file (such as a document or photo) over the folder.
2. When the folder highlights, release your mouse to drop the file inside.
3. Double-click the folder anytime to see what's inside.

Renaming Files and Folders

To rename:

1. Click once on the file or folder.
2. Wait a moment, then click the name again (not double-click).
3. Type the new name and press **Return**.

Deleting Unwanted Items

To remove a file or folder:

1. Click it once.
2. Press the **Delete** key or **right-click > Move to Trash**.
3. To permanently delete, open the **Trash** from your Dock and click **Empty**.

Tip: Be sure you don't need the file before emptying the Trash!

Searching for Files

Can't find a file? Use the **Search bar** at the top right of any Finder window:

1. Type part of the file name or a keyword.
2. Finder will show matching results immediately.

Using Tags for Organization

Tags help you color-code or label important items:

1. Right-click any file and hover over **Tags**.

2. Choose a color or add a custom label like "To Print" or "Important".

3. Tagged items can be found by clicking the color/tag name in the Finder sidebar.

SECURITY, PRIVACY & MAINTENANCE

Security essentials: Protecting against malware and viruses

Your MacBook is designed with safety in mind, but taking a few extra precautions can help protect your personal information and keep your device running smoothly. Let's go over some simple, friendly steps to guard against malware (unwanted software) and viruses.

1. Understanding Malware and Viruses

- **Malware** is software designed to harm your computer or steal information. Think of it like a pest that can sneak into your home if you're not careful.
- **Viruses** are a type of malware that can spread from one device to another. Just as you wouldn't leave your door open, it's important to keep your digital "doors" secure.

2. Keep Your Software Updated

Software updates are like routine checkups for your MacBook. They fix problems and patch up vulnerabilities.

- **macOS Updates**: Regularly update your operating system by clicking the Apple icon () and selecting **System Preferences** > **Software Update**. Install any available updates.
- **App Updates**: Make sure your apps, including security tools, are updated through the **App Store**.

3. Use Built-In Security Features

Your MacBook comes with several built-in features designed to protect you:

- **Gatekeeper**: This feature prevents untrusted apps from running. It only allows software from the App Store or identified developers.
- **XProtect**: A built-in antivirus that checks for known malware automatically.
- **Firewall**: A tool that monitors and controls incoming connections. Turn it on by going to **System Preferences > Security & Privacy > Firewall** and clicking **Turn On Firewall**.

4. Install Reliable Antivirus Software

While Macs are generally secure, installing a trusted antivirus program can add another layer of protection:

- **Choose a well-known antivirus program**: Look for software with good reviews and a reputation for reliability.
- **Regular Scans**: Set the antivirus to run scans automatically. This helps catch potential threats early.
- **Keep it Updated**: Like your MacBook, the antivirus software needs updates to recognize the latest threats.

5. Be Cautious with Downloads and Email Attachments

Malware often sneaks in through downloads and email:

- **Download from Trusted Sources**: Only download software or files from websites you know and trust.
- **Email Attachments**: Be careful with attachments, especially from unknown senders. If something looks odd, it's best not to open it.
- **Pop-Up Alerts**: Don't click on suspicious pop-up ads. They can sometimes be tricks to get you to download harmful software.

6. Practice Safe Browsing

When you're online, a few habits can help keep your MacBook safe:

- **Avoid Suspicious Websites**: Stick to reputable sites. If a website looks unusual or too cluttered with ads, it might not be safe.
- **Use a Secure Browser**: Safari is designed to protect your privacy, but make sure you update it regularly.
- **Don't Share Sensitive Information**: Only enter personal details on secure websites (look for "https://" at the beginning of the address).

7. Regular Backups with Time Machine

Backing up your data won't stop malware, but it will protect you if something goes wrong:

- **Set Up Time Machine**: Connect an external drive and let Time Machine back up your data regularly. This means even if your MacBook is affected, your files are safe.
- **Store Backups Safely**: Keep your backup drive in a safe place, separate from your computer.

8. What to Do If You Suspect an Infection

If you think your MacBook might have malware or a virus:

1. **Disconnect from the Internet**: This helps prevent any further potential damage or spread.
2. **Run a Full Antivirus Scan**: Let your antivirus software check every corner of your MacBook.
3. **Check Activity Monitor**: Open **Applications > Utilities > Activity Monitor** to see if any unfamiliar processes are running. If you're not sure about a process, search online or ask a trusted tech-savvy friend.
4. **Seek Professional Help**: If you're still worried, consider contacting Apple Support or a professional technician.

Understanding and managing privacy settings

1. What Are Privacy Settings?

Privacy settings control what information your MacBook shares with apps, websites, and even with Apple itself. Think of these settings like curtains on your windows—when closed, they help protect your personal space.

- **Location Services**: Decides which apps can know where you are.
- **Contacts, Calendars, and Photos**: Determines which apps can access your personal files.
- **Analytics and Improvements**: Lets you choose whether to send usage data to Apple to help improve your products.

2. Accessing Privacy Settings

1. Click on the **Apple menu ()** at the top left of your screen.
2. Choose **System Preferences**.
3. Click on **Security & Privacy**, then select the **Privacy** tab.

This is your control center for all privacy options on your MacBook.

3. Managing Specific Privacy Settings

Location Services

- **Enable/Disable**: Check the box to allow apps to use your location, or uncheck to turn it off.
- **Choose Apps**: Click on the lock icon (bottom left) and enter your password. Then, select or deselect the apps you trust to access your location.

Tip: It's a good idea to only enable location services for apps you use regularly and trust.

Contacts, Calendars, and Photos

- **Select Each Category**: On the left sidebar, click **Contacts**, **Calendars**, or **Photos**.
- **Review Permissions**: You'll see a list of apps that want access to these areas. Check or uncheck each one based on your comfort level.

Tip: For sensitive data like your contacts, only allow access to apps that you really need.

Analytics and Improvements

- **Decide on Sharing**: In the **Privacy** tab, scroll to **Analytics & Improvements**.
- **Toggle Options**: You can choose whether to share Mac usage data with Apple. Unchecking this option means less data is shared, but it might affect personalized recommendations.

4. General Privacy Best Practices

- **Keep Your Software Updated**: Updates often include improvements to privacy and security.
- **Regularly Review Permissions**: Check your privacy settings every few months to make sure only trusted apps have access.
- **Be Cautious with New Apps**: When you install a new app, it may ask for access to personal data. Think about whether the app really needs this information before you grant permission.
- **Use Strong Passwords**: Good passwords help keep your accounts secure, and you can manage these settings in the **Security & Privacy** section under **General**.

Secure password management

Managing your passwords is like keeping the keys to your home safe. A strong, secure password helps protect your personal information and prevents unauthorized access. Here's a friendly, step-by-step guide on how to manage your passwords securely on your MacBook.

1. Why Strong Passwords Matter

- **Protection**: A strong password is like a sturdy lock on your door. It helps keep your private information secure from unwanted visitors.
- **Prevention**: With the right password, you prevent others from easily guessing or accessing your accounts.

2. What Makes a Strong Password?

A strong password usually includes:

- **Uppercase and Lowercase Letters**: Mixing these makes it harder to guess.
- **Numbers**: Adding numbers makes your password even more secure.
- **Special Characters**: Symbols like !, @, or # add extra protection.

Imagine your password is like a recipe—more ingredients make it unique and hard for someone else to duplicate.

3. Creating a Strong Password

Here's a simple method to create a strong password:

1. **Pick a Phrase**: Choose a sentence that is meaningful to you, for example, "I love sunny days in the park."
2. **Use the First Letters**: Convert the phrase into initials (e.g., `ILSDitP`).
3. **Add Numbers and Symbols**: Spice it up by replacing some letters with numbers or symbols. For example, `IL0v3$unnYd@Yz!`

Remember, the goal is to create something memorable yet difficult for others to guess.

4. Storing and Managing Passwords

You don't have to remember every single password on your own. Here are a few ways to keep them safe:

- **Password Manager**: Consider using a password manager. This is a secure app that stores all your passwords in an encrypted (locked) format. Some popular options are 1Password, LastPass, or even Apple's own iCloud Keychain.
    - **iCloud Keychain**: It comes built into your Mac and safely stores your passwords, credit card information, and Wi-Fi passwords. To enable it:
        1. Go to **System Preferences > Apple ID > iCloud**.
        2. Check the box next to **Keychain**.
- **Writing Them Down**: If you prefer a pen and paper, write your passwords in a small notebook and keep it in a secure place at home. Just be sure not to leave it where others can easily find it.

5. Changing and Updating Passwords

Regularly updating your passwords is a good habit, just like changing the batteries in your smoke detector.

- **Set Reminders**: Consider changing your important passwords (like your email and bank accounts) every few months.
- **Avoid Reuse**: Try not to use the same password for multiple accounts. If one gets compromised, others might be at risk.

6. Two-Factor Authentication (2FA)

For extra security, consider enabling Two-Factor Authentication (2FA) on your accounts.

- **How It Works**: After entering your password, you'll also need to enter a code sent to your phone or another trusted device.
- **Why It Helps**: This means even if someone figures out your password, they still can't access your account without that second piece of information.

Recognizing and avoiding scams

1. Common Types of Scams

- **Email Scams (Phishing):** These are messages that appear to be from a trusted company, asking you to click a link or provide personal information. They often contain spelling mistakes or unusual language.

- **Phone Scams:** Unsolicited calls where the scammer pretends to be from a bank or government agency, urging you to share sensitive details or transfer money.

- **Pop-up Ads and Fake Websites:** Unexpected pop-up windows or websites claiming your computer is infected, asking you to download software or click a link.

- **Online Shopping Scams:** Offers for products that seem too good to be true, often leading to a request for payment without delivery of the promised item.

2. Red Flags to Watch Out For

- **Urgency and Pressure:** Scammers often create a sense of urgency, such as warning you that your account will be locked or you'll miss out on a limited-time offer.

- **Requests for Personal Information:** Be cautious if someone asks for passwords, credit card numbers, or Social Security numbers unexpectedly.

- **Unusual Email Addresses or Phone Numbers:** Check the sender's email address or phone number. If it looks odd or doesn't match the official website or contact information, it might be a scam.

- **Poor Grammar or Spelling:** Many scam messages contain obvious errors. While not all mistakes indicate a scam, they can be a warning sign.

- **Too-Good-to-Be-True Offers:** If an offer seems unbelievably generous or a deal is way below market value, it could be a scam.

3. Safe Practices to Avoid Scams

- **Verify Before You Trust:** If you receive an email or phone call asking for personal information, don't reply immediately. Contact the company or person directly using a trusted phone number or website.

- **Avoid Clicking on Suspicious Links:** If you're unsure about a link in an email or pop-up, don't click it. Instead, type the official website address directly into your browser.

- **Use Two-Factor Authentication:** Adding a second layer of security to your accounts makes it much harder for scammers to gain access, even if they have your password.

- **Keep Your Software Updated:** Regular updates help protect your MacBook from security vulnerabilities that scammers might exploit.

- **Educate Yourself:** Familiarize yourself with common scams. Many banks and government agencies provide resources on their websites that explain what to watch out for.

4. Real-Life Example

Imagine receiving an email that claims you've won a free vacation. The email asks you to click a link and enter your personal information to claim your prize. It sounds exciting, but before you get too eager, consider these questions:

- Do you really remember entering any contest?
- Is the email address from a reputable source?
- Does the message contain spelling mistakes or urgent language?

If the answer is "no" to any of these questions, it's best to ignore the email or delete it.

5. What to Do If You Suspect a Scam

- **Don't Respond:** If you think a message or call might be a scam, do not reply or click on any links.
- **Report It:** Many companies and government agencies have dedicated websites for reporting scams. For example, in the U.S., you can report scams to the Federal Trade Commission (FTC).
- **Talk to Someone:** If you're ever unsure, ask a trusted friend or family member for their opinion. Sometimes a second pair of eyes can help spot a scam.

Regular MacBook maintenance (software updates, cleaning storage)

1. Software Updates

Why Updates Matter:

- **Improved Security:** Updates fix security gaps and protect against new threats.
- **Better Performance:** They help your MacBook run faster and smoother.
- **New Features:** Updates often add useful features or improvements to existing ones.

How to Check for Updates:

1. Click the **Apple icon ()** in the top-left corner of your screen.
2. Choose **System Preferences**, then click **Software Update**.
3. Your MacBook will check for available updates. If any are found, you'll see a message asking you to install them.
4. Click **Update Now** to start the process. Your MacBook might restart during the update—this is completely normal!

Tip: It's a good idea to check for updates once a month. You can even enable automatic updates in the Software Update settings so you never miss an important fix.

2. Cleaning Storage

Over time, your MacBook can accumulate lots of files that you no longer need—like old documents, duplicate photos, or apps you rarely use. Cleaning up your storage can free up space and help your Mac run more efficiently.

Steps to Clean Your Storage:

- **Review Your Files:**
    1. Open **Finder** (the blue smiling face icon in your Dock).
    2. Navigate to folders like **Downloads, Documents**, and **Desktop**. Look for files you no longer need.
    3. Drag unwanted files to the **Trash**.

- **Empty the Trash:**
    1. Click the **Trash** icon in your Dock.
    2. Right-click or click the **Empty** button to permanently delete the files. (Make sure you really don't need them before doing this!)

- **Manage Large Files:**
    1. In **Finder**, go to **File > Find** and click the + button to set search criteria.
    2. Choose **File Size** and set a size (like larger than 100 MB) to locate large files.
    3. Review these files and decide if you want to delete or move them to an external drive.

- **Uninstall Unused Apps:**
    1. Open the **Applications** folder in Finder.
    2. Look for apps you rarely or never use.
    3. Drag them to the **Trash** and then empty the Trash.

Tip: Consider setting aside a regular time—maybe once every few months—to review and clean your storage. This small routine can help keep your MacBook running smoothly and free up space for new files.

ACCESSIBILITY & EASE OF USE

Accessibility features overview (VoiceOver, dictation, magnification, text-to-speech)

Your MacBook is designed with everyone in mind, including those who may need a little extra help when using technology. Accessibility features ensure that your device is easy to use, whether you need assistance with reading, speaking, or simply adjusting the display. In this section, we'll explore some of the most useful accessibility tools available on your MacBook: VoiceOver, Dictation, Magnification, and Text-to-Speech. Each feature is explained in a clear, step-by-step way so you can try them out and see what works best for you.

1. VoiceOver

What is VoiceOver?

VoiceOver is a built-in screen reader that speaks aloud what is on your screen. Think of it as a friendly guide that reads text for you, so you can know what's happening even if the text is too small or if you prefer listening.

How to Turn On VoiceOver:

1. Click the **Apple menu ()** in the top-left corner.
2. Select **System Preferences**, then click **Accessibility**.
3. In the left sidebar, click **VoiceOver**.
4. Check the box next to **Enable VoiceOver**. You can also press Command + F5 to turn it on or off quickly.

Using VoiceOver:

- Once activated, your MacBook will read aloud items on the screen.
- You can navigate by using the arrow keys, and VoiceOver will announce each item as you move.
- To learn more about using VoiceOver, click the **Open VoiceOver Utility** button in the Accessibility settings. This utility offers tips and shortcuts for getting the most out of this feature.

2. Dictation

What is Dictation?

Dictation allows you to speak instead of typing. It converts your spoken words into text, which is great if you find typing on a keyboard challenging.

How to Enable Dictation:

1. Open **System Preferences**.
2. Click on **Keyboard**, then select the **Dictation** tab.
3. Click **Turn On Dictation**.
4. Choose your preferred language and, if you like, enable the option for enhanced dictation. This option lets you dictate offline and provides real-time feedback.

Using Dictation:

- To start dictating, simply place your cursor in any text field (like a document or email) and press the **Fn (Function) key** twice (or use your chosen shortcut).
- Speak clearly into your MacBook's microphone. You'll see your words appear on the screen.
- When you're done, press the **Fn key** again to stop dictating.

Tip: Practice speaking naturally and slowly at first. Over time, you'll become more comfortable, and your MacBook will get better at understanding you.

3. Magnification

What is Magnification?

Magnification helps you see smaller text and images more clearly by zooming in on the screen. It's similar to using a magnifying glass on paper.

How to Enable Magnification:

1. Open **System Preferences** and click **Accessibility**.
2. In the sidebar, select **Zoom**.
3. Check the box next to **Use keyboard shortcuts to zoom**. You can also choose other zoom options like scroll gesture with modifier keys.

Using Magnification:

- To zoom in, press `Option + Command + =` (equal sign). To zoom out, press `Option + Command + -` (minus sign).
- You can also hold the **Control key** and scroll with two fingers on your trackpad to zoom in and out.
- Explore additional settings in the Zoom options to adjust the zoom style and maximum zoom level to suit your needs.

4. Text-to-Speech

What is Text-to-Speech?

Text-to-Speech converts written text into spoken words, which is perfect if you'd like to listen to articles, emails, or documents instead of reading them.

How to Set Up Text-to-Speech:

1. Go to **System Preferences** and select **Accessibility**.

2. In the left sidebar, click on **Spoken Content** (or **Speech** in older versions of macOS).

3. Check the box that says **Speak selected text when the key is pressed**.

4. Choose a voice from the list provided. You can adjust the speaking rate to make it slower or faster, depending on what's most comfortable for you.

Using Text-to-Speech:

- To use this feature, select the text you want to be read aloud.

- Press the designated key combination (often `Option + Esc`) to start the speech.

- Your MacBook will read the selected text out loud. If you want to stop, simply press the same key combination again.

Customizing your MacBook for optimal comfort

1. Adjusting Visual Settings

Screen Brightness and Contrast:

- **Brightness:** Adjust the screen brightness using the brightness keys on your keyboard (usually marked with a sun icon) or through **System Preferences > Displays**. A well-lit screen reduces eye strain.

- **Contrast and Color:** In **System Preferences > Accessibility > Display**, you can increase contrast or reduce transparency, making text and images easier to see.

Text Size and Resolution:

- **Text Size:** Increase the text size in apps like Mail or Safari by using the zoom function (Command + +) or adjusting the settings within each app.
- **Screen Resolution:** Choose a scaled resolution that makes items on your screen larger by going to **System Preferences > Displays > Scaled**.

2. Customizing Audio Settings

Volume and Alerts:

- **Adjust Volume:** Use the volume keys on your keyboard to set a comfortable sound level.
- **Sound Effects:** In **System Preferences > Sound**, you can choose different alert sounds and adjust how loudly they play, ensuring you never miss an important notification.

Accessibility Audio Options:

- **Mono Audio:** For those who prefer hearing the same sound in both ears, enable Mono Audio in **System Preferences > Accessibility > Audio**.
- **Subtitles and Captions:** If you watch videos, turn on subtitles or closed captions by checking the relevant options in the app you're using or in **System Preferences > Accessibility > Captions**.

3. Personalizing the Desktop

Organizing Your Workspace:

- **Desktop Background:** Choose a calming or meaningful image as your wallpaper by right-clicking on your desktop, selecting **Change Desktop Background**, and picking an image that suits your taste.

- **Dock Settings:** Customize the Dock by adjusting its size, magnification, and position. Go to **System Preferences > Dock** to move the Dock to the side of the screen if that feels more natural, or to increase its size for easier clicking.

Using Stacks and Folders:

- **Stacks:** Use Stacks to automatically organize files on your desktop by kind (such as documents, images, or PDFs). Right-click on the desktop and select **Use Stacks**.
- **Folders:** Create folders in Finder to keep your important documents, photos, and apps grouped together, making your digital space tidy and easy to navigate.

4. Configuring Input Devices

Trackpad and Mouse Preferences:

- **Trackpad Settings:** Adjust the trackpad sensitivity and gestures by going to **System Preferences > Trackpad**. You can enable or disable gestures like swiping between pages or using three fingers to switch apps.
- **Mouse Options:** If you prefer a mouse, customize its tracking speed and scrolling direction in **System Preferences > Mouse**.

Keyboard Customizations:

- **Key Repeat Rate:** In **System Preferences > Keyboard**, adjust how quickly a key repeats when held down. A slower rate can prevent accidental repeated letters.
- **Shortcut Customization:** Familiarize yourself with or customize keyboard shortcuts to streamline your workflow. For example, you can create shortcuts for common tasks like opening your favorite apps.

5. Adjusting Notifications and Alerts

Managing Notifications:

- **Notification Center:** Open the Notification Center by clicking the date/time in the top-right corner. From here, you can see and manage notifications from different apps.
- **Customize Alerts:** In **System Preferences > Notifications**, you can choose which apps can send you notifications and customize how they appear. This helps reduce distractions and ensures that you only receive alerts that matter most.

6. Personalizing Accessibility Features

VoiceOver, Dictation, and More:

- **Fine-Tune Accessibility Settings:** Revisit the accessibility options (VoiceOver, Magnification, Text-to-Speech, etc.) in **System Preferences > Accessibility** to adjust their speed, volume, and other settings according to your comfort.
- **Custom Shortcuts:** Set up custom keyboard shortcuts for turning on accessibility features. This allows you to quickly access these tools when needed.

Adjusting audio settings for better clarity

1. Accessing the Sound Settings

1. **Click the Apple Icon ():** In the top-left corner of your screen, click the Apple menu.
2. **Open System Preferences:** From the drop-down menu, select **System Preferences**.
3. **Select Sound:** Click on the **Sound** icon. This will open the audio settings where you can adjust output and input devices.

2. Adjusting the Output (Speaker) Settings

Choose the Right Output Device:

- **Default Speakers:** Your MacBook's built-in speakers are usually selected by default. If you're using external speakers or headphones, select the appropriate device from the list.
- **Balance Control:** Under the **Output** tab, you'll find a slider labeled **Balance**. This lets you adjust the sound between the left and right speakers. If one side feels louder or clearer than the other, move the slider until the sound is even.

Enhance Sound Quality:

- **Volume Level:** Adjust the overall volume using the slider. Aim for a level that's comfortable for you—loud enough to hear clearly, but not so loud that it causes discomfort.
- **Sound Effects:** Some sound effects can enhance clarity. You might want to experiment with different system sounds (like alert tones) in **System Preferences > Sound > Sound Effects** to find the ones that are easiest for you to hear.

3. Adjusting the Input (Microphone) Settings

If you use your MacBook for dictation or video calls, a clear microphone input is just as important.

- **Select the Right Microphone:** Under the **Input** tab, choose your built-in microphone or an external one if you have it connected.
- **Input Volume:** Use the slider to set the microphone's sensitivity. Speak normally and adjust until your voice is picked up clearly without too much background noise.
- **Ambient Noise Reduction:** Many MacBooks have an option to reduce ambient noise. Ensure that this is enabled so that the microphone focuses on your voice rather than background sounds.

4. Using Accessibility Audio Options

For additional clarity and customization, your MacBook offers extra accessibility audio settings:

- **Mono Audio:** If you have difficulty distinguishing between left and right channels, you can enable Mono Audio. This combines the audio channels into one, ensuring you hear the full sound through both ears. Find this option in **System Preferences > Accessibility > Audio**.

- **Adjusting Alerts:** In the **Sound Effects** tab, you can change the alert volume and choose different tones. Sometimes a sharper, clearer sound is easier to notice, especially if background noise is present.

- **Equalizer Settings:** While macOS doesn't have a built-in equalizer in the System Preferences, some media apps (like Music) offer equalizer settings. Adjust these settings to enhance vocal clarity or boost certain frequencies that you find easier to hear.

5. Tips for Better Audio Clarity

- **Use Quality Headphones or Speakers:** Sometimes, the clarity of audio is affected by the quality of the output device. Consider investing in a pair of good quality headphones or external speakers if you frequently listen to music or watch videos.

- **Minimize Background Noise:** For the best experience, try to use your MacBook in a quiet environment. This not only improves clarity but also helps the built-in microphone capture your voice more accurately.

- **Regularly Update Your Software:** Keeping macOS updated ensures that any improvements or bug fixes related to audio are applied to your system.

TROUBLESHOOTING COMMON ISSUES

Basic troubleshooting tips (freezing, restarting, battery issues)

1. What to Do If Your MacBook Freezes

A frozen MacBook means it becomes unresponsive—you can't click, type, or move anything.

Try This First:

- **Wait a Moment:** Sometimes your MacBook is just "thinking." Give it a few seconds—especially if you were opening a large file or app.
- **Force Quit the App:**
  1. Press `Command + Option + Esc` (think of this as your emergency escape!).
  2. A window will pop up showing a list of open apps.
  3. Select the one that says "Not Responding" and click **Force Quit**.
  4. Close the window and return to your desktop.

If everything is frozen (even the mouse or keyboard), you may need to restart your Mac.

2. Restarting Your MacBook

Restarting clears temporary glitches and gives your system a fresh start.

How to Restart Normally:

1. Click the **Apple icon ()** in the top-left corner.
2. Select **Restart**.
3. If prompted, choose whether to reopen windows or not. (If your Mac froze recently, unchecking "Reopen windows" can help avoid repeating the issue.)

If Your Mac Is Completely Unresponsive:

- Press and hold the **power button** (usually in the top-right corner of the keyboard) until the screen goes black.
- Wait a few seconds, then press the power button again to turn it back on.

Tip: Restarting your Mac once a week can help prevent slowdowns and minor bugs.

3. If Your MacBook Is Running Slowly

Over time, having too many apps open or not enough storage space can slow things down.

Quick Fixes:

- **Close Unused Apps:** Use Command + Q to fully quit apps you're not using.
- **Restart Your Mac:** A simple restart can work wonders.
- **Check Storage Space:**
    1. Click the Apple icon > **About This Mac**.
    2. Go to the **Storage** tab and see how much space is free.
    3. If your storage is nearly full, consider deleting large files or moving them to an external drive.

4. Troubleshooting Battery Problems

If your MacBook battery drains quickly or doesn't charge properly, here are some helpful checks:

Basic Checks:

- **Is the Charger Plugged In Properly?** Make sure the charging cable and adapter are fully inserted and connected to power.
- **Check the Charging Indicator:** A lightning bolt icon in the menu bar means your MacBook is charging.
- **Inspect the Charger:** Try using a different wall socket or a different charger if you have one.

Battery Health:

1. Click the **Apple icon > System Settings > Battery**.
2. Look for **Battery Health**.
3. If it says **"Service Recommended,"** the battery may be aging and need replacement.

Improve Battery Life:

- **Lower Screen Brightness.**
- **Close Unused Apps.**
- **Turn Off Bluetooth and Wi-Fi** when not needed.

Tip: Avoid keeping your MacBook plugged in 24/7. Let the battery cycle occasionally (charge and discharge) for better long-term health.

5. General Tips to Keep Things Running Smoothly

- **Update Software Regularly:** Updates often fix bugs and improve performance.
- **Shut Down at Night (Once in a While):** Letting your Mac rest is healthy—just like you!

- **Use Safe Mode (Advanced Tip):** If you're having repeated issues, restarting in Safe Mode can help identify the problem. Hold the **Shift key** while restarting to enter Safe Mode.

Solving common internet/Wi-Fi problems

1. First, Check If It's Really a Wi-Fi Problem

Before troubleshooting your MacBook, check a few basics:

- Are **other devices** (like your phone or tablet) also having trouble connecting? If so, the issue may be with your Wi-Fi network or modem—not your MacBook.
- Is your **Wi-Fi router/modem** plugged in and powered on? Look for blinking lights on the box.
- Is your **internet provider** having an outage? You can check by calling them or visiting their website (if you have access on another device).

If it seems to be just your MacBook that's having issues, let's move on to fixing it.

2. Common Wi-Fi Problems and How to Fix Them

Problem 1: "No Wi-Fi Connection" or "No Internet"

Solution: Reconnect to Your Wi-Fi Network

1. Click the **Wi-Fi icon** in the top-right menu bar.
2. If Wi-Fi is off, click **Turn Wi-Fi On**.
3. Click your home network name from the list.
4. Enter the **Wi-Fi password** if prompted, then click **Join**.

If you're already connected, but the internet doesn't work:

- Try turning Wi-Fi **off**, wait a few seconds, then turn it back **on** again.
- Restart your MacBook (Apple menu > Restart).
- Restart your modem/router by unplugging it from the wall, waiting 30 seconds, then plugging it back in.

Problem 2: Slow Internet

Solution: Try These Simple Steps

- Move closer to your **Wi-Fi router**—walls and distance can weaken the signal.
- Close apps or browser tabs you're not using—they may be using internet in the background.
- Pause any large downloads or updates (like a software update or video download).
- Restart your MacBook and router.

If it's always slow in one spot of your home, you might need a **Wi-Fi extender** to boost the signal in that area.

Problem 3: Keeps Disconnecting from Wi-Fi

Solution: Forget and Rejoin the Network

1. Go to **System Settings > Wi-Fi**.
2. Click the small **"i" icon** next to your Wi-Fi network name.
3. Click **Forget This Network**.
4. Now go back and reconnect by choosing the network and re-entering your password.

This can help your MacBook "start fresh" with the connection.

Problem 4: Connected to Wi-Fi But No Internet Access

This usually means your Mac is talking to the Wi-Fi router, but the router itself isn't connected to the internet.

Solution: Restart Your Equipment

1. Turn off your MacBook.
2. Unplug your **modem/router**, wait 30 seconds, then plug it back in.
3. Wait for the lights to come back on (this may take 1–2 minutes).
4. Turn your MacBook back on and reconnect to Wi-Fi.

If the problem persists, call your internet provider. The issue may be with the service line to your home.

3. Helpful Mac Tools for Diagnosing Wi-Fi

Use Wireless Diagnostics:

1. Hold the **Option key** on your keyboard.
2. Click the **Wi-Fi icon** in the top-right menu bar.
3. Select **Open Wireless Diagnostics**.
4. A tool will appear to scan your connection. Just follow the on-screen instructions.

This built-in tool can help find problems automatically!

4. General Wi-Fi Tips for a Strong Connection

- **Keep your MacBook updated**: Software updates can fix hidden Wi-Fi bugs.
- **Avoid signal blockers**: Try not to place your router behind thick walls or near metal furniture.

- **Secure your network**: Use a strong password so neighbors don't slow your internet by connecting without permission.
- **Rename your Wi-Fi network** (optional): This can help you quickly identify your home network, especially in apartment buildings with many nearby routers.

How and when to get professional help (Apple Support, AppleCare)

1. When to Ask for Professional Help

Here are some signs that it may be time to reach out to Apple Support or visit an Apple Store:

- You've tried restarting or troubleshooting but the issue keeps happening.
- Your MacBook won't turn on, freezes constantly, or displays unusual error messages.
- Your battery drains very quickly or won't charge at all, even after trying a different charger.
- There's a hardware issue—such as a broken key, cracked screen, or a damaged charging port.
- You suspect a virus or malware and your MacBook isn't acting like it normally does.
- You're simply unsure about something and would feel better talking to someone knowledgeable.

Remember: There's no harm in asking for help early, especially if it gives you peace of mind.

2. What Is Apple Support?

Apple Support is Apple's free help service. You can speak to a real person by phone, chat online, or make an appointment to get in-person help at a local Apple Store or authorized repair shop.

How to Contact Apple Support:

1. **Visit the Website**

   Go to https://support.apple.com

   From here, you can:

   - Search for help articles
   - Start a live chat
   - Schedule a phone call or in-store visit

2. **Use the Apple Support App**

   Download the **Apple Support app** from the App Store. It's a simple tool that helps you get personalized support and make appointments quickly.

3. **Call Apple Directly**

   If you prefer talking to someone right away, call Apple Support:

   - In the U.S., the number is **1-800-MY-APPLE (1-800-692-7753)**

4. **Visit a Local Apple Store**

   You can book a **Genius Bar appointment** at an Apple Store through the Apple Support website or app. They'll help diagnose and fix your MacBook on-site, and many minor repairs can be done the same day.

3. What Is AppleCare?

AppleCare is Apple's extended warranty and support plan. It provides additional coverage beyond the standard one-year warranty.

AppleCare+ includes:

- **Extended hardware coverage** for up to 3 years
- **Battery service** if your battery holds less than 80% of its original capacity
- **Coverage for accidental damage** (like drops or spills), with a small service fee
- **Priority access to Apple experts** for help over the phone or chat

How to Check If You Have AppleCare:

1. Click the **Apple menu () > About This Mac**.

2. Click **More Info**, then select **Service**.

3. You'll see whether your MacBook is covered under warranty or AppleCare.

If you don't have AppleCare yet, you may still be eligible to buy it within 60 days of purchasing your MacBook.

4. What to Bring or Know Before Getting Help

When visiting an Apple Store or repair center:

- Bring your **MacBook** and **charger**.
- Bring your **Apple ID** and **password**.
- Be ready to explain the issue clearly (write down symptoms or when it started if helpful).
- Back up your important files, just in case the MacBook needs to be reset or serviced.

ADVANCED TIPS & TRICKS

Using iCloud: Backup and synchronization

1. What Is iCloud?

Think of iCloud as a secure digital storage room in the sky. Instead of keeping all your photos and documents only on your MacBook, iCloud saves them online, so you can:

- Access them from anywhere
- Automatically back up important data
- Sync your information across all Apple devices

2. Setting Up iCloud on Your MacBook

1. Click the **Apple menu ()** in the top-left corner.
2. Go to **System Settings** or **System Preferences** (depending on your macOS version).
3. Click on your **Apple ID** at the top of the settings window.
4. Select **iCloud** from the sidebar.

From here, you can choose what information to store and sync with iCloud. Options include:

- **Photos**
- **Contacts**
- **Calendars**
- **Notes**
- **Safari (bookmarks and browsing history)**
- **iCloud Drive** (for documents and files)

■ **Tip:** Make sure you're signed in with the same Apple ID on all your Apple devices to keep everything in sync.

3. What Is iCloud Drive?

iCloud Drive is your online folder that lives inside the Finder on your Mac. Anything you save here is automatically backed up and available on your other Apple devices.

To Access iCloud Drive:

- Open **Finder** (the blue face icon).
- Click **iCloud Drive** in the left sidebar.
- You can drag and drop files into this space just like you would with any regular folder.

This is a great place to store documents you want to access from your phone, tablet, or another Mac.

4. Using iCloud for Photos

If you turn on **iCloud Photos**, your entire photo library is stored safely online and kept up-to-date across your devices.

To enable it:

1. Go to **System Settings > Apple ID > iCloud**.
2. Click **Photos**, then enable **iCloud Photos**.

Benefits:

- New photos automatically appear on all devices.
- You can delete photos from one device, and they'll be removed everywhere (careful with this!).
- You won't lose photos if your device is ever lost or damaged.

📺 *Tip: If you're low on storage space, you can choose to store "optimized" (smaller) versions on your Mac, with the full-size images saved in iCloud.*

5. Backup Using iCloud

Your MacBook doesn't back up to iCloud in the same way an iPhone or iPad does, but you can still back up important files.

Here's how to protect your data using iCloud:

- **Documents and Desktop Backup:**
    1. Go to **System Settings > Apple ID > iCloud**.
    2. Click **iCloud Drive > Options**.
    3. Turn on **Desktop & Documents Folders**.

This will automatically upload everything on your Desktop and in your Documents folder to iCloud Drive.

- **App Data and Settings:** Many apps also use iCloud to back up their data—such as Notes, Reminders, Safari bookmarks, and Calendar events.

6. Managing iCloud Storage

By default, Apple gives you **5GB of free storage**. You can check how much you're using and upgrade if needed:

1. Go to **System Settings > Apple ID > iCloud**.
2. Click **Manage** next to **iCloud Storage**.

From here, you can:

- See which apps are using the most space
- Delete old backups or files you no longer need
- Upgrade to a larger storage plan (like 50GB, 200GB, or 2TB) for a small monthly fee

💡 *Tip: If you take lots of photos or videos, you may eventually need to upgrade your storage plan. It's affordable and can give you peace of mind.*

7. Syncing Across Devices

If you also use an iPhone or iPad, turning on iCloud ensures everything is synced:

- Contacts added on your iPhone will appear on your MacBook
- Notes written on your MacBook will show up on your iPhone
- Bookmarks saved in Safari stay in sync on all devices

Just make sure you're signed in to the same **Apple ID** on each device and have iCloud enabled for the same apps.

Managing downloads and installing apps

1. Understanding Downloads: Where Do They Go?

When you download something from the internet—like a file, photo, or document—it goes into a special folder on your Mac called **Downloads**.

How to Find the Downloads Folder:

- Click the **Finder** icon (the blue smiling face in the Dock).
- In the left sidebar, click **Downloads**.
- Everything you've downloaded recently will be here.

💡 *Tip: Think of the Downloads folder like a "mailbox" for files coming in from the internet. It's a good idea to check it regularly and clean it out when it gets full.*

2. Downloading Files from the Internet

Example: Downloading a PDF or Picture

1. Visit a trusted website (like a library or email provider).
2. Click a **Download** link or button.
3. The file will automatically download and appear in your Downloads folder.
4. Click the file to open it (macOS will automatically use the right app, like Preview for PDFs).

■ *Be careful where you click! Only download from trusted websites you know and recognize. If a file seems suspicious or unexpectedly downloads, delete it right away.*

3. Installing Apps from the App Store

The **Mac App Store** is the safest and easiest way to get new apps. All apps there are reviewed by Apple for security.

How to Install an App from the App Store:

1. Click the **App Store** icon in the Dock (it looks like a blue circle with an "A").
2. Use the **Search bar** in the top-left to find the app you want (e.g., "Zoom," "Spotify," or "Solitaire").
3. Click **Get** or **Install** (you may need to enter your Apple ID password or use Touch ID).
4. The app will download and appear in your **Applications** folder or **Launchpad**.

To open your new app, just click it in **Launchpad** (the rocket ship icon in your Dock), or find it in Finder under **Applications**.

4. Installing Apps from Other Trusted Sources

Sometimes you may want to download an app directly from a trusted website—like Google Chrome or Zoom.

How to Install an App from a Website:

1. Go to the **official website** of the app (for example, `www.google.com/chrome`).
2. Click **Download**.
3. Once downloaded, open the file in your **Downloads** folder. Most apps come as a `.dmg` (disk image) file.
4. A window will appear showing the app icon and a shortcut to the Applications folder. **Drag the app into the Applications folder**.
5. Once it's copied, you can eject the installer by clicking the **Eject** icon in Finder.

■ *Never download apps from unfamiliar pop-ups or ads. Always go to the official site or use the App Store.*

5. Managing Installed Apps

How to Find Installed Apps:

- Click **Launchpad** to see all your apps in one place.
- Or open **Finder > Applications** for a list view.

How to Delete Apps You Don't Use:

From Launchpad:

1. Click and hold on an app icon until it starts to jiggle.
2. Click the **X** that appears (only works for App Store apps).
3. Click **Delete**.

From Finder:

1. Go to **Applications**.
2. Drag the app to the **Trash**, then empty the Trash to fully remove it.

6. Keeping Downloads Organized

If your Downloads folder is getting crowded, here's how to tidy up:

- **Move files** you want to keep into organized folders (e.g., Documents, Photos, or a custom folder like "Recipes").
- **Delete old or unused downloads** by right-clicking and selecting **Move to Trash**.
- **Sort by date** in the Downloads folder to quickly find the newest items.

Customizing your MacBook's appearance and notifications

1. Changing Your Desktop Wallpaper

Your desktop background is the first thing you see when your Mac starts. You can choose from Apple's built-in images or use your own photos.

How to Change Your Wallpaper:

1. Right-click anywhere on the desktop and select **Change Desktop Background**.
2. The **System Settings** window will open with wallpaper options.
3. You can choose from:
   - Apple's default images (scenic views, patterns, etc.)
   - **Photos** from your own library (great for family pictures!)
4. Click the one you want, and it will instantly change your background.

■ *Tip: If you use a family photo, make sure it's high-quality so it doesn't appear blurry.*

2. Adjusting the Dock

The Dock is the row of icons at the bottom (or side) of your screen that lets you quickly open apps.

To Customize the Dock:

1. Go to **System Settings > Desktop & Dock**.
2. Here, you can:
    ○ **Change the Dock's size** (make it bigger or smaller).
    ○ **Turn on magnification**, which enlarges icons as you hover over them.
    ○ **Move the Dock** to the left, right, or bottom of the screen.
    ○ **Auto-hide the Dock** so it only appears when you move your mouse to the edge.

● *Tip: Keep only the apps you use often in the Dock for a cleaner look.*

3. Choosing Light or Dark Mode

macOS lets you choose between **Light Mode** (brighter appearance) and **Dark Mode** (darker background, easier on the eyes at night).

To Switch Modes:

1. Open **System Settings > Appearance**.
2. Choose **Light**, **Dark**, or **Auto** (which switches based on time of day).

● *Many people find Dark Mode more comfortable in the evening.*

4. Changing Icon Size and Text on the Desktop

If the items on your desktop look too small (or too large), you can easily resize them.

How to Change Icon Size:

1. Right-click on your **Desktop**.
2. Choose **Show View Options**.
3. Use the slider to increase or decrease **icon size** and **grid spacing**.
4. You can also choose a **larger text size** for the file names.

👓 *This is especially helpful for visibility and comfort if you prefer bigger text.*

5. Customizing Notifications

Notifications are messages from your apps (like Mail, Calendar, or Messages) that appear on your screen. You can control how and when they show up.

To Manage Notifications:

1. Open **System Settings > Notifications**.
2. You'll see a list of apps that send notifications.
3. Click any app (e.g., Calendar or Mail) to customize:
   - **Alert Style**: Choose how the alert appears (banner, alert, or none).
   - **Sounds**: Turn sound on or off for that app's notifications.
   - **Preview**: Choose whether to show message previews (useful for privacy).

⬤ *Tip: If you don't want to be disturbed, turn on **Do Not Disturb** or **Focus Mode** (more below).*

6. Using Focus Mode

Focus Mode helps you reduce distractions by controlling when notifications appear.

To Turn On Focus Mode:

1. Click the **Control Center icon** (two toggle switches) in the top-right corner of your screen.
2. Click **Focus**.
3. Choose a mode, like:
    - **Do Not Disturb**: Blocks notifications temporarily.
    - **Sleep** or **Work**: Customize for specific routines.

You can schedule Focus modes or allow certain people (like family members) to still reach you during these times.

Siri: Getting the most from your personal assistant

1. What Is Siri?

Siri is a voice-activated assistant that responds to your questions and commands. You can ask Siri to perform tasks like:

- Setting reminders or alarms
- Sending messages
- Opening apps or websites
- Giving you weather updates
- Answering general questions ("What time is it in London?")

The beauty of Siri is that you don't need to know complicated commands—just talk to her like you would to a friend.

2. How to Turn On Siri

To check if Siri is enabled on your MacBook:

1. Click the **Apple menu ()** > **System Settings** (or **System Preferences**).
2. Select **Siri & Spotlight** from the sidebar.
3. Toggle **Ask Siri** to **On**.
4. You can also enable **Listen for "Hey Siri"** so you don't have to click anything—just speak the wake phrase!

💡 *If you're using Siri for the first time, your MacBook may walk you through a quick setup process.*

3. How to Use Siri

Once Siri is turned on, you can activate her in a few ways:

- **Say "Hey Siri"** (if enabled)
- Click the **Siri icon** in the top-right menu bar (a circular waveform)
- Press and hold the **Command + Spacebar** keys

When Siri is listening, you'll see a waveform and hear a chime. Simply ask your question or give a command.

Examples of Things You Can Say:

📓 "Remind me to take my medication at 8 p.m."

📫 "Send an email to Sarah."

📓 "What's on my calendar today?"

♨ "What's the weather like tomorrow?"

🔊 "Turn up the volume."

♟ "Open Safari."

🔍 "Search for photos from my trip to Florida."

4. Making Siri Work for You

Siri gets better the more you use her. Here are a few ways to make the most of this helpful assistant:

- **Ask Follow-Up Questions:** Siri remembers the context of your last question. For example:
  1. You: "What's the weather in New York?"
  2. Then: "How about on Friday?"
- **Use Natural Language:** No need for commands like a robot—just speak normally.
- **Personalize Siri's Voice and Language:**
  1. Go to **Siri & Spotlight** in System Settings.
  2. Choose your preferred **Siri voice** (male or female, with regional accents).
  3. You can also change the language if you prefer to speak in another one.

5. Privacy and Siri

Siri is designed to respect your privacy. You can manage what Siri listens to or remembers:

- Go to **System Settings > Siri & Spotlight > Siri & Dictation History**.
- You can choose to delete Siri's history or limit certain features.

🔒 *Siri processes most information anonymously and gives you full control over your settings.*

Tips to extend battery life and optimize performance

Your MacBook is a powerful machine—but just like a car runs better with care and attention, your MacBook also performs best when it's well looked after. In this section, you'll learn simple, practical tips to help your battery last longer and keep your MacBook running quickly and smoothly over time.

1. Adjust Screen Brightness

The screen is one of the biggest power users. Lowering your brightness can make a noticeable difference.

How to Adjust It:

- Use the **brightness keys** on your keyboard (sun icons), or
- Go to **System Settings > Displays** and slide the brightness bar.

☀ *Tip: Keep the brightness as low as is comfortable for your eyes—especially indoors.*

2. Turn Off Bluetooth and Wi-Fi When Not in Use

If you're not using Bluetooth accessories or don't need to be connected to Wi-Fi, turning these off saves power.

- **Bluetooth:** Go to **Control Center** (top-right corner) > **Bluetooth** > Toggle Off.
- **Wi-Fi:** Same as above—just tap **Wi-Fi** and turn it off if you're not online.

✈ *Bonus Tip: Use "Airplane Mode" when traveling or working offline.*

3. Close Unused Apps and Browser Tabs

Running lots of apps or browser tabs in the background can slow things down and drain your battery.

What to Do:

- Close any windows or tabs you're not using.
- Press Command + Q to quit an app completely (not just close the window).

💡 *Check which apps are using the most power by clicking the battery icon in the menu bar.*

4. Use Safari Instead of Other Browsers

Safari is optimized for macOS, which means it uses **less energy** than other browsers like Chrome or Firefox.

- If you want the best performance and battery life while browsing the web, stick with Safari when you can.

⬤ *Plus, Safari includes helpful features like Reader Mode and built-in privacy tools!*

5. Update Software Regularly

macOS updates often improve battery efficiency and performance.

To Update:

- Go to **Apple Menu () > System Settings > Software Update**
- Click **Update Now** if one is available

🛠 *Think of updates like a tune-up—they help your MacBook run more efficiently.*

6. Use Energy Saver Settings

Apple offers built-in settings that help extend battery life.

How to Access:

1. Go to **System Settings > Battery**.
2. Under **Battery Health**, enable **Optimized Battery Charging** to slow battery aging.
3. Set your display to turn off after a short period of inactivity (e.g., 5 minutes).
4. Turn on **Low Power Mode** if your battery is running low or you want to stretch it further.

⚡ *Low Power Mode reduces background activity while still allowing you to work.*

7. Reduce Visual Effects

Fancy animations may look nice, but they use extra power and system resources.

To Turn Them Off:

- Go to **System Settings > Accessibility > Display**
- Enable **Reduce Motion** and **Reduce Transparency**

🐦 *Your MacBook will still look great—just a little more efficient.*

8. Monitor Storage and Free Up Space

A nearly full hard drive can slow your MacBook down.

To Check Storage:

- Go to **Apple Menu () > About This Mac > Storage**
- Click **Manage** to review and delete large or unused files

📁 *Clean storage means faster performance and a happier MacBook!*

BONUS

 BONUS #1: Recommended Apps & Resources

Your MacBook can do so much more than just check emails or browse the internet. It's a powerful tool that can support your well-being, help you stay organized, and even keep you entertained or learning something new. In this bonus section, I've put together a list of simple, trustworthy apps and resources that are great for seniors. Whether you're looking to stay healthy, get more done, or just enjoy your downtime, there's something here for you to try—no tech expertise required.

Health & wellness apps

🧘 Health & Wellness Apps Staying healthy—physically and mentally—is easier when you have the right tools at your fingertips. These apps can help you keep track of your well-being, practice relaxation, and stay active from the comfort of home.

1. MyFitnessPal Tracks your meals, calories, and nutrition. It helps you develop healthier eating habits with ease. ■ Available on: Web and mobile
2. Medisafe A medication reminder app that helps you take the right dose at the right time. Great for managing prescriptions. ■ Available on: iPhone (can sync with Mac reminders or calendar)
3. Calm A beautifully designed app for guided meditations, breathing exercises, and calming music—ideal for reducing stress and improving sleep. ■ Available on: Mac (via web) and iPhone
4. Pacer Turn your iPhone into a step counter. It's simple, no-frills, and helps you stay active with walking goals. ■ Use with: iPhone + Mac syncing

■ Productivity Tools From writing documents to organizing your day, these apps help you stay sharp and get more done—without being overwhelming.

1. Evernote Take notes, create to-do lists, and save articles to read later—all in one place. Easy to organize and sync across devices. ■ Available on: Mac and iPhone

2. Google Calendar Plan your appointments, birthdays, and events. You can set reminders that pop up right on your screen. ■ Available on: Web, syncs with Mac Calendar

3. Notion A modern, customizable workspace where you can keep notes, recipes, daily logs, or even start journaling. It's surprisingly beginner-friendly with templates to guide you. ■ Available on: Mac (free version is enough for most users)

4. Grammarly A helpful writing assistant that corrects spelling and grammar in emails, documents, or web forms. ■ Available on: Safari extension or Mac app

■ Entertainment & Educational Apps Whether you love movies, want to learn something new, or just enjoy a good puzzle, these apps will keep your days engaging and fun.

1. YouTube Watch videos on any topic—cooking, travel, history, music, and more. You can even search for "beginner tutorials" to learn new skills. ■ Available on: Safari or as a web shortcut

2. Netflix Stream movies and shows (requires a subscription). Easy to browse, pause, and resume watching on your own schedule. ■ Available on: Web and iPhone

3. Libby by OverDrive Borrow eBooks and audiobooks from your local library—free of charge. Perfect for avid readers and audiobook lovers. ■ Use your library card to get started. ■ Available on: Web and iPhone

4. Lumosity A brain-training app with daily games to help improve memory, attention, and problem-solving. Fun and rewarding! ■ Available on: Mac (via browser) and iPhone

5. Khan Academy Free educational videos on everything from art history to computer basics. Great for lifelong learners. ■ Available on: Safari (just visit www.khanacademy.org)

📕 BONUS #2: Quick Reference Keyboard Shortcuts

Easy-to-follow tables of essential keyboard shortcuts:

👆 Basic Everyday Shortcuts

Shortcut	What It Does
Command + C	Copy selected text or item
Command + V	Paste copied text or item
Command + X	Cut (remove and copy) selected text or item
Command + Z	Undo your last action
Command + A	Select all items or text in a window
Command + S	Save your current document

◼ Finder & File Shortcuts

Shortcut	What It Does
Command + N	Open a new Finder window
Command + Delete	Move selected file to Trash
Command + Shift + N	Create a new folder
Command + I	Get info about a selected file or folder
Spacebar	Quick Look (preview) a file

⊕ Browsing the Web (Safari or Any Browser)

Shortcut	What It Does
Command + T	Open a new browser tab
Command + W	Close the current browser tab
Command + L	Jump to the address/search bar
Command + R	Reload (refresh) the current page
Command + Click Link	Open a link in a new tab

■ Switching & Managing Apps

Shortcut	What It Does
Command + Tab	Switch between open apps
Command + Q	Quit the current app

Command + H	Hide the current window
Command + M	Minimize the current window

 Printing, Screenshots & System Shortcuts

Shortcut	What It Does
Command + P	Print the current page or document
Command + Shift + 3	Take a screenshot of the full screen
Command + Shift + 4	Take a screenshot of a selected area
Command + Spacebar	Open Spotlight search (find files or apps)
Control + Command + Power	Restart your MacBook

■ Calendar, Mail & Notes Shortcuts

Shortcut	What It Does
Command + N	Create a new event, email, or note (depends on app)
Command + R	Reply to an email
Command + Shift + R	Reply to all in an email conversation
Command + F	Search for text in a note or email
Command + K	Add a link in Notes or Mail

🔍 Spotlight & Search Shortcuts

Shortcut	What It Does
Command + Spacebar	Open Spotlight (search your Mac)

Command + F	Find a word or phrase in the open window
Command + Option + Esc	Force quit an unresponsive app

📌 *Tip: Spotlight can help you find files, launch apps, or even do simple math—try typing "123 + 456" in it!*

■ System Navigation & Control

Shortcut	What It Does
Control + Up Arrow	See all open windows (Mission Control)
Control + Down Arrow	See windows for the current app
Command + Shift + Q	Log out of your user account
Control + Command + Q	Lock your screen quickly
Option + Command + Esc	Force quit a frozen app (like Ctrl + Alt + Delete)

● Text Editing & Formatting (In Pages, Notes, Mail, etc.)

Shortcut	What It Does
Command + B	Make text bold
Command + I	Italicize text
Command + U	Underline text
Command + T	Open the Fonts panel
Command + Shift + >	Increase text size
Command + Shift + <	Decrease text size

👍 *These are perfect for formatting emails or writing documents.*

● Memory-Boosting Tip:

Try this method to remember the basics:
C is for **Copy**,

V is for **Paste**,

Z is for **Undo**,

Q is for **Quit**.

Practice just 2–3 shortcuts a week and before long, you'll be zipping around your MacBook like a seasoned pro!

www.ingramcontent.com/pod-product-compliance
Lightning Source LLC
LaVergne TN
LVHW081700050326
832903LV00026B/1851